What Goes into a Butterfly?

By

Sunil Rajagopal

This is a work of poetry. Some experiences, places and conversations have been recreated from the author's hazy memory. Everything else is purely a figment of his imagination. Any resemblance to actual people (living or dead), events, institutions etc., is purely coincidental or fictitious.

First Edition: February 2019
Printed in India

ISBN: 978-93-87269-90-3

Cover Design: Prashant Gurav
Illustrations:Sunil Rajagopal

STORYMIRROR
Stories that reflect you

Publisher: StoryMirror Infotech Pvt. Ltd.
145, First Floor, Powai Plaza,
Hiranandani Gardens,
Powai, Mumbai- 400076, India

Web: www.storymirror.com
Facebook: www.facebook.com/storymirror
Twitter: https://twitter.com/story_mirror
Instagram: https://instagram.com/storymirror

If I show you
what moves me,
will you see
what I see?

If I tell you
where I go,
will you then
walk with me?

- SR

Contents

Part-1
Quiet Roads & Hidden Nooks

1.

Just a Road

Ask not where I turn and lead,
Near, far or whether you shall bleed;
Ask not where I begin and end,
Others may await beyond my bend;
Ask not who shall follow you,
Those that stay will be but a few;
To write my story, that is your load,
I am just here you see, just a road.

2.

Around a Bonfire

The wind came with a knife
and the chill with a blanket,
the night came to whisper
about the moon gone looking
for stars lost in the fields.

The blaze in the middle
craves the centre stage,
it sings and it sways,
it mutters and it smokes,
telling tall tales.

When I stared long enough
for a spell to be cast,
from the flames arose
demons and dragons
and other fabulous beasts.

3.

Mawphlang

Year after year
the grasslands march
fuelled by fire
and axe blades sharp
till the hills stand bare
and trees are a fable,
all but here at Mawphlang
at the edge of a knoll
rolling up and sliding down
where a hoary army
holds them back,
a stand of deep woods dark!
It is a place of fear
and ancient rites,
Ferns and Lilies
and gravestones moss,
Oak and Birch
and Rudraksh beads!
The sky is green
and so is the earth,
water grows from every root,
magic brews in every shoot!

The air is thick with whispers
of a long-lost tongue
and the earth is bound
by a sisterhood!
If you walk long enough
you may just meet
old men in the forest
grinning toothless in rock
with faces lichen hard;
If you walk far enough
an elder Oak may
open up its trunk
to give you shelter;
You may walk with care
under the ancient ones,
but none may leave
with any part of them.

4.

Dara Shikoh's Tomb

The Dead lie callous;
Light does not always fall on
those that need it most.

5.

The Fig Trees of Humayun's Garden

Four stand the Pilkhan
older than us all,
Four against the years
and the vagaries of time;

Four in a corner
of a garden of paradise,
Four in a square
in a field of eights;

Four in the shade
of the red bald dome,
Wearing crowns and beards
grander than the Khan's;

Four for the Mughals
and the Company's men,
Four for us in the Hind
and those yet to come;

Four against the sun
for the birds and mice,
Four they still live
in the garden of the dead.

6.

The Train Stops at Dharampur

The little lights dim
one by one,
Half past nine
and the hills are in bed;
Who's still up
but the wind in the pines
and the drowsy rain
crooning on the roof?
A glow worm trundles
tooting through the trees,
Half past nine
and it is time
for the last train to Kalka.

7.

The Ruins of Mandu

Time knows no rest,
All days must walk west;

Kings and their deeds gather dust,
Their swords taken by rust;

Beauty of Queens is as frost,
Melting into grass and lost;

The towers of men fallen apart,
Amidst gnarled baobabs looming apart;

Only the rain and wind remain
To whisper their tales again.

8.

At the Pass

Nothing stirs
but the wind in a red rag,
only a trident stands guard!
To learn the truth of Shiva,
we must live where he sleeps,
Go where he walks
in lonely places
Where no trees march
and from snows spring
young rivers.

9.

Thar

Where winds melt the sun,
Where the devil is in dust,
A land without end.

10.

Shepherd

Come to me, children,
from sparse grass and rock,
Even in my winter
this sickle and crook are for you.

There are more lines
on my face than there are
paths running on these hills,
You are safe with me.

11.

Children on the Beach

We fear not eventide,
in Mother's lap we play and
Our dreams are still young.

12.

A Song Stuck in My Head

a song, a dream,
it's an endless loop
a road to fall
off the edge of the map

a life, a time
too heavy a load
a laugh, a tear,
a drop of hope

a brush, a stroke
to paint a winding road
a tree, a turn,
a temple, a grove

a smith, a fire
a burning knife
a foot, a yard,
a glass of leaping tea

a shack, a crowd,
it's a flaming wok
a light, a house
they watch the purple sun

the salt, the swells,
it's a fishy smell
a boat, an oar
to chase after the shoals

a whistle, a cry
to shoot at goal
a leap, a roll,
a spray of sand

a hawk, an owl,
a night, a day
it's all the same
all they want is to fly

a cloud, a shaft
it's rain on the march
a cow, a priest,
a row of coconut fronds

a kite, a bell,
it's the darkest blue
a tune, a prayer
for the last time today

a song, a dream
in an endless loop
a road to fall
off the edge of the map.

13.

White Dog Bully

I am the white dog
they call Bully,
I'll wait at the gate
come morning light.

Trot with me
down to the stream,
up the hillock
where the berries grow;

Slide with me
down the red mud slopes,
into the pool
between the rocks;

Roam with me,
nose to the earth,
ears to the wind
tasting everything;

Roll with me
in the coarse grass,
in the shady slush
loved by the thrush;

Track with me
below the trees,
The deer drink here!
The pigs dig here!

Run with me
amidst the wildflowers,
one leap behind
a frenzy of quail!

Sit with me
on the dusty terrace
Watching the sun fade
into the night;

I am the white dog Bully
you know well,
I'll wait for you
come morning light;

Come with me,
on the morrow
I go to meet
the leopard in his lair.

14.

They Come to Kashi

They come here in droves
to sip sweet tea by the stoves
and feed grain to the doves;

They walk in lanes of grime
in this city older than time,
where even the barbers rhyme;

They learn how to weave
between what the cows leave,
and hear history through a sieve;

They watch the great river flow,
easing creases in every brow,
Taking everything with it slow;

When all that's left is a sigh,
They come here to die
where the smoke rises to the sky.

15.

Night Landing

I wake in a cloud,
Lightning quivering at the wingtips.
Tonight, I am the one in the sky,
gazing down
on the sea of night and floating on it,
An island of glittering stars.

But these cannot be stars -
They are too many,
too close.
Yellows and Reds standing in circles,
swimming in grids & lines.
They have no twinkle,
no magic;
They offer no wisdom,
no hope;
This is no distant world of old,
These are but the harsh lights
of the city.

16.

A Long Way Home

Dreams of endless roads,
open flats and snaking ghats,
one with wind and rain!

When they ask why, I
tell them of home far away,
green hills by the sea!

Every forest a
different deep, so much to
see - I cannot stay!

17.

In the End, the Sea

Where goes the sun at
long day's end? To douse his red
fire within the Sea.

Where goes the monsoon
and her clouds after their dance?
To drink from the Sea.

Where goes the river
after meandering course?
To sleep in the Sea.

Where goes the Hilsa
tired from swimming up the flow?
To die in the Sea.

Where goes the sailor
who returned with his bounty?
To live in the Sea.

There may come a time
when I too shall return home,
To be with the Sea.

Part-2
In Every Little Drop

1. A Better Poem

I sat down
to make a poem
from the falling rain,
when down swam
a little spider
weaving strands
of the tiniest drops
with his magic silk
in a precious garland
and I wrote no more.

2.

What Goes into a Butterfly?

What goes into a butterfly?
A slice of Sky
with a pinch
of Earth;
Toss it in Wind,
Sprinkle some Rain,
Dip it in Honey
and let it fly!

3.

Web

Things of beauty both
fragile flight of butterflies
and their death by silk.

4.

Feather

Neem leaves weep
for their fallen brother;
He once could fly,
this brown feather.

5.

Bubble

A bubble in a birdbath
in a balcony of a house
under a tree;
in the bubble
in the birdbath
the balcony, the house and the tree;
brief, but beautiful!

6.

Old Brooding Tree

I sat in the lap of
an old brooding tree
till my years turned grey
in search of god -
Maker of rain,
Giver of food,
Builder of homes,
Root of all rivers,
Stem of our air,
Haven at all times,
Shield for the meek,
Spear for the strong,
The power that binds the earth
and on its crown bears the sky!
But alas! I sat there
till my time came
but never did once
God cross my path.
When at last
I lay down to die,
Then, and only then,
did I see
the spreading might
of the old brooding Tree.

7.

Her Spirits

Go where the wind blows,
Fall when the earth calls,
Rise when the sky wills,
Let the fires burn,
Walk in the rain,
They are you,
Woman.

8.

Listen to Them

Have you heard
an owl fly by?
Like the morning hush,
A thousand butterflies
taking wing!

Have you heard
the falling dew?
Like popping peas,
the patter of tiny
running feet!

Have you heard
a bluebird sing?
Like a winter's noon,
a glob of honey
dripping down!

Have you heard
a tiger roar?
Like the darkened moon,
a rumble of waterfall
thundering past!

Have you heard
a tree's quiet sigh?
Like the silent stars,
the whisper of a hand
soft on your hair!

9.

Gulmohur & Alstonia

I am in love with
two ladies next door, maybe
one loves me more.
The cool prim one,
she stands very still
be it rain or wind;
In Fall I fell for
the alluring scent laced
in the dark of her mane.
The other stands coy
in her robe of ferns and
red burns her summer hair.
She sways to the breeze,
weeps in the rain
and in winter mourns the sun.
One smiles at me from afar,
while the other ruffles soft
my hot tangled hair.

Often, they stand
hand in hand, quiet beside as
I watch the world sleep.
But I am just one,
among many more that find
joy in their midst.
I am in love with
these ladies next door, maybe
one loves me more.

10.

Fall

A tree without leaves
is not without life, so too
fate of fallen men.

Do not grieve for the
flame trees that sprinkle their leaves,
a red spring awaits.

11.

Frangipani Flowers

Drunk with beauty they
mocked the passing rain and fell
laughing to the earth.

12.

It

It watches over
the whole world and yet,
in each little drop, it lives.

13.

Oru Appoopan Thadi / Silk Cotton seed

I am Grey-beard Just-born,
No wings but windborne,
I peek into nooks all along
for a muddy bed to live long.

14.

Cycles

The light of a star
through the canopy sewn,
A tree reaching far
from where it was sown;
A heavy crown
so wearily worn,
A dry leaf brown
in the wind blown.

15.

Time and Starlight

On those black nights
when I wish I could
go back in murky time
and wonder how,
I gaze at the deep sky
and its denizens who are gone
long before I can
catch their starlight.

16.

Redeemer

A crow dangles stiff
in the mulberry spread,
Wings spread open and wide
rocking softly side to side,
A hawk has had its fill
and there's not a drop to spill.
A lone black quill
in the red air still,
Wafting this way and that
with nowhere to be at,
Till a squirrel thought it best
to take it home to her nest.

17.

The Last Firefly

A firefly winked,
then shimmered his love
alone in the dark
and got not one flash
for all his troubles;
Just as he grew quiet
to cry himself to sleep
as the last of his kind,
the Sky opened wide
to hurl a sizzling bolt across.

18.

The Many Meanings of Dew

What is fresh dew but
pearls for the morning grass, sweet
honey for fireflies!

****

Sailing in the fog,
Spider's ships of glistening
dew and silken threads!

****

In clear dew and leaves,
In warm sun and trees, beats the
Heart of the Forest.

****

19.

Coppice

One grey morning after
the wind ran amok,
the old feather-leaved tree
took a tumble to the earth;
They took their time
sawing its branches
and fair smooth trunk,
when evening came
only the roots lay there alone.
A new spell of rains came rustling
and bustling through the streets,
and when the week was done
the old tree woke from the dead!
A hundred saplings rising,
growing from its roots
daring the wind to come
try its luck once and more.

20.

Colour of the Hills

Red the earth
Bleeding from the darts
Of relentless clouds
That stole the blue
From tired skies;

On the slopes clinging
To the Sholas hunched
Wet in the folds
Of the mountains of rain,
In the clear water
that trickles from its darkness,
A spell is cast
Once in a blue bloom
From the beating heart
Of the goddess under the trees;

A little flower awakens
in years of dozens
to conquer the slopes,
Shoulder to shoulder with
green grass and fern
hard rock and mist
To return the blue
to the open skies.

Part-3

On Long Walks

1.

A Deer in the Mist

Still as the morning
he stood in the gloom;
Slivers of mist drooped
over his haunch,
A glint of dew
in his spreading crown,
Warm breath puffing
from his cold wet nose;
Crack went a twig
beneath my feet -
I looked up and
the stag was gone.

2.

That Time of the Year

That time of the year
when even wee little brooks
call themselves rivers;
roaring loud and surging past,
bursting banks and running brown.

3.

Without an Audience

Where the stream trickles
from a bank of yellow reeds,
There the deer come to drink
in the shadow of the trees;
Where the hills are brown
with grass burnt by the sun,
There is a little ledge perched
watching over the valley;
Where the peacock prances
with his blue fan spread,
There is no one to hail
the artist on his stage.

4.

A Man in a Hurry

On a hot day in Puri,
running from a priest
who claimed his price
for a prayer I didn't want,
Hopping over a bull's tail
past the holy slush around,
straight into a man in a hurry!
He glared and snapped—
Where do you think you are going?
I was quiet, and he snarled—
Who do you think you are?
I stepped away quietly,
for truly, I did not know.

5.

Pie Dog

I stumbled on a street
teeming with the zealous
Rushing to meet their everyday;
No one stopped, no one smiled,
They did not care;
Like a million ants
they swirled around and
yet I stood alone
till I felt his soft wet
nose behind my knee;
Kind brown eyes smiled
at me from a fuzzy face,
A kindred soul, a solace
amidst faceless strangers.
Alas! It is he they want to stone.

6.

The Sky-Road to Tungnath

To doubting hearts and trembling knees
trudging up the sky-road to
the shrine on the mountain
the finches sing, loud and clear!
Can just a little April cold
and a door of dead wood shut
make the lord of the peaks go
striding down to Ukhimath?
Can't you hear the powdery snow
crackling on the spring road
and the wind howling in
the great Griffon's wings?
Don't you see the rainbows caught
by the Monal in his glittering robe
and the sweet fires blazing
in the rhododendron wood?

Feel the will of juniper and oak
bearing time on their bent old backs
and hordes of wildflower
conquering the slopes?
Bit by bit feel your way up
like the Pika by her whiskers,
to see the thundercloud crown
the old tower of rock you came for.

7.

Birder by the Lake

Tell me friend, for what do you linger?
Wintering fowl and their murmuring wings.

Tell me friend, why do you shiver?
My nose is cold and the breeze has stings.

Tell me friend, where are your winged folk?
My hands are asleep and so are the ducks in the mire.

Tell me friend, do you see the water smoke?
Yes! Morning has come to set the lake afire!

8.

Death in the Ditch

Two brown hawks roving
the sky splashed ruddy blue,
fingers tip to tip.

Up and up they rise
in lazy maddening loops
on the sultry breeze.

Can they see the stiff
stag and his flies in the ditch?
Did they see him fall?

Can they smell my dread
of that tail twitching in the grass,
branded black on gold?

They are climbing still,
touching a rare cloud, too far
now to watch my fate.

9.

Sunsets Three

From the foot of the hill
I saw the sun go down
behind the black leaved palms,
Then once more it
hid in the leafless trees
as I scrambled up slope,
At the top at last
as I caught my breath
The sun set again,
this third time in the clouds.

10.

Forgotten Street

Walking down a forgotten street
listening to the birds tweet,
the music of rain on leaves,
dragonflies dancing their magic weaves.

11.

The Importance of Walking

No pleasure like that
in the company of friends
and long walks with them,

No treasure like that
of memories born afresh
along long-lost roads.

12.

River's End

Red flowers and dead lamps
stranded on a crowded crook
in the river's bend;

Boulders on the bed
hiding a feeble dribble
where the river ebbed;

A place of tall grass
and boats swimming stolen sand,
at the river's end.

13.

Ali in the Sea

I went to see
Old Man Ali
who sleeps in the Sea
till the romping tide
turns at its time;

Old Man Ali—
they call him Haji
for he flew across the Sea
at Mecca to be free
and from his worries flee;

From the dirty city
I walked up the levee
that swims through the Sea
for all who wish to see
Old Man Ali;

A rumble of cloud
A grey heavy shroud
hung like a kite
with its string caught tight
in the tower of Ali's light;

Old men trip
Young girls skip
A wave of people slip
bunched upon the levee
lashed by the Sea;

Sweat in every crease
runs with the drizzle,
A warm briny breeze
licks and nuzzles
in all that hustle;

When I paused for an imp
then a lady with a limp,
A wave came leaping
the spray flew slapping—
they came from Ali;

And he whispered,
Just Keep Walking!

14.

Dancing Girl of Dungarpur

I once went walking
with goats in the scrub
in Dungarpur
where there are dunes in the east
and dunes elsewhere;
On a hard track trudging
between rows of cactii
I saw a dusty girl dancing
with the evening's fire
perched on her head;
She twirled on the dune
like a flame in the wind
spinning and flickering,
A lone girl whirling
with her laughter and her hair
and the desert in her eyes;
The dunes and the twilight
they were hers by right,
but she saw me coming
and hid behind her veil,
she saw me coming
and danced no more.

15.

Winter Line

I am cold and lost
in a dizzy of eagles
rousing the sky
and stand here bound
to the tread of dirt and stone;
But far afield I see
across the shaggy beard of Deodar
past the wrinkled cheek of hills
beyond the mirrored fields
molten river snakes
sullen fog and burning cities,
A spear of a line thrown
russet and black
threading the bending sky
to the rising earth
end to end;
The eagles have become clouds
and I cannot follow,
I'll just keep going
to that searing line,
on and on
to world's end.

16.

A Tiger's Tale

When the fire burns long
and friends run out of songs,
I sometimes share
a tale of peril
of when I went to see
a leopard in a pond
with a twenty rupee torch
and a bottle of coke
but met instead
a tiger in a bush
who roared at me
and made the earth shiver
as I stood in his way
to the cows in town;
It's a fine old yarn
and they'd love it more
if I didn't forget the part
where I ran for my life.

17.

Stranger

I froze at the edge
of the swarming mob
buzzing and snapping around
festival stalls sticky sweet,
My belly did a twist
and I stopped in fear
of drowning in their midst
for I cannot swim;
Until I felt a soft, strange hand
clasp mine tight
and say in an urgent voice,
It's only till you get me across.

Part-4: Birds in Their Sky

1. Marsh Harrier

An army of ramrod reeds
bunched alone,
row upon row
marching in the gloom;
Till the fog conjured
a ghost from its heart,
a harrier probing
on languid wings;
A little bit of sun
glinting on her head,
the reaper swept low
sowing fear in her wake;
It started as a ripple
running in the reeds,
and then grew in to
one churning swell.
A pandemonium of birds
bloomed from within,
Teals and geese, crakes
and drakes, all at once.

A tilt of the wings,
a twist of the tail and
the slayer slipped quiet
in to the mob running blind.
It waned like it waxed,
to a sudden chilly hush,
the harrier sat down
to breakfast in the reeds.

2.

The Banasar Falcon

In the belly of the ochre sky
Grew a tumour of a fort
Broken and brooding
Muttering black Gorkha spells;
From its sullen depths
Blew a turpentine wind
Armed with ice-picks
To mine salt from eyes;
Around this darkness
flickered pines like beacons
While a maze of swifts
mothed around their green flame;
Till there flew a swift
scythe-winged and impossibly huge
from inside the old stones,
Opaque as their past;
It rose and rose
above the pines
on an invisible stairway
till it was swift no more;
For a heartbeat it hung there
like a bow;

A bow, a cross bow taut,
straining,
before it plunged,
Slowly at first,
then heavy as an anchor
Tearing through the wind;
The torrent of swifts heaved,
heaved and splashed,
Then parted to let the dagger pass
and melted into dusk
before their hunter planed out;
The falcon returned to its stones,
The pines glimmered a little less.

3.

Jacobin Cuckoo

A Jacobin bird
rummaging in the bushes,
Cucking and cooing
in his black coat and white shirt
and a dandy peaked black cap.

He sailed across the
wide sea in the vanguard of
swirling dark cloud banks;
When he sings of rain - believe!
Ten days hence, the monsoon lands.

4. Shikra

There is a red-eyed devil
hidden in the Neem leaf rush,
It is in his fear that
the tree stopped talking.
White of brow with
dread in his eyes,
Smoke blue cloak over
a rust streaked breast,
Death in his talons and
the wind in his wings,
No one stirs under his
watch in this leafy world!
The squirrels are mute,
the pigeons are frozen,
the tailor has vanished and
the lizard changed its colours,
So quiet is panic when
the sparrowhawk hunts.

5.

Demoiselles

They swept by at dusk—
a kiss of wind, a rush of
wings, a whiff of cold!

A passing whim to
chase their paths across the sky,
questing endless springs!

6.

Wader

A shadow quiet,
painting the still water with
ripples running gold.

7.

An Owl's Wisdom

I see day as well
as you do, I sleep only
to avoid some fools.

8.

Vulture

Barn door wings creaking
in the hush of stoic peaks,
drifts a lone vulture.

9.

Carcass Dump

The ground is soft with
muscle and marrow
and broken bone,
The air is ripe with
death and decay
and buzzing flies,
Here walk those
that come to see
the vultures feed.

10.

Sudden

It is light on the hill
but the wooded valley
lies gloomy and still,
it is a hunter's alley;

A hungry silver owl
peering from a bamboo brush
felt nothing foul,
till death's oncoming rush;

A hawk fell from the sky
knives drawn for her brother,
The screaming wind, her warring cry,
his life but hers to smother!

In the bamboo they scuffled
as one bird blend,
Fine feathers were ruffled
before the red end.

11.

The Peacock Dances Alone

One thousand blue eyes,
a peacock dancing alone
under the Neem tree.

Mee-yow! Mee-yow! calls
the mournful peacock and yet
vainly pirouettes.

None may halt for his
rare charms, for peacocks dance
under every tree.

12.

Evolution

Eagles soar, falcons
stoop, gulls glide and owls ambush;
To each their own wing!

13.

The Brothers Raven

Down from the shoulders
of the all-seeing mountain
flew a pair of ravens
to meet me in the snow;
Those glassy black eyes,
they see in the snow,
they see me in the snow
in the shadow of the mountain;
Those glossy dark wings—
they are not black
but night and green and inky blue
dabbed on a ripple of purple hue;
I asked them their name
and they said with a strut,
Korrrakk! and Gurrraaw!
and we be brothers!
They may have beards
and gravelly tongues
but aren't quite my forefathers;
From the blind-sided mountain
they come not to haunt,
they bear no blessings,
it's just my biscuits they want.

14.

The Seagulls are Coming

A boat, a shadow of a boat,
On the dead river sleeping
Poison Black!

The sun, a bled-out sun,
Lost in a void cursed
Deathly Grey!

A flight of gulls, luminous gulls
Burning up the fog
Ember White!

Gulls, a blizzard of gulls,
Kindling a fire
Molten Gold!

A frenzy, a melee, all around the boat,
Brewing up a spray
And the river lives again!

15.

Tyto Alba

The night sleepless
Dimmed,

By the road endless
Rushing,

On Friday breathless
Flushed;

The night restless
Shushed,

By an owl weightless
Silvering,

A wing song soundless
Whispered.

16.

We Went Looking for a Golden Eagle

Up and around
the young brown mountain
till we found
a land without trees
and piles of cotton
close enough to kiss,
just too far to touch!
A shadow passed,
blotting the blue
skimming the scree,
trailed by a scream!
We stood in thrall
to the queen on the mountain
who wears light
her crown of gold
and the weight of the sky!
It was but a moment
but who will tell that
to the little army standing tall
on the back of my neck?

17.

Starling

One bright star fell from above
Clutching tight to a piece of night,
They fell through the pink of dawn,
Through the red of dusk
Into emerald fields
Rippling under a violet sky
And broke into shimmering bits,
They fell and they broke and flew
as a dancing flock of common starlings.

Part-5
Lost & Found

1.

In Search of Lost Forests

There once was a forest
spreading from the sea
whose roots held time
as the years grew moss,
A dark place of memory
where I was lost and found;
Where now is that forest
that grew within me?
Where are those giants
that held up the sky and
the swords of morning that
sliced their misty robe?
Who stole the laughter
from its spry creeks,
hushed the whisper of
many rising wings?
How did the meadows lose
their dewy sheen and
the quicksilver feet
that singed their grass?

Where are the fell shadows
which lurked within its deep?
Where is the firefly that
danced within its heart?
Where is the forest which
once sheltered my dreams?

2.9

When the Sea calls

My glass is clouded;
In this driving rain, a whiff -
of the salty sea!

Listen to the rain
Like many running ripples,
Like gulls on the wing!

Sailor I am not,
Nor fisher or diver deep;
Yet I hear her call!

It rolls and it tugs,
This rising swell within me;
Deep, soft, all at once!

Her shores are not mine,
Nor to her waves I belong;
Yet for them I yearn!

When the sea beckons
from afar, I close my eyes;
She roars within me!

3.

Teacher on the Bus

When the first day of school
was still the first day of monsoon,
my head dripping with rain
I would run to my bus.

She would always be there
waiting on the step,
a smile for my troubles
and a towel for my head.

What lessons were taught,
the lay of my school,
the rains of my city,
all that is lost to me now.

But still burning in my mind
is a kind-eyed teacher
waiting on the bus
with a towel and her smile.

4.

I Let the Firefly Go

When days grew too bleak and stark,
I clad my world in velvet night.
I kept walking led by my lamp
through paths unseen but not alone.
This steady lamp, it showed me the way
when the moon and stars fell asleep.
The lamp was dear, my only warmth
when all around was cold and dank.
Then I saw the little firefly,
a fallen star gleaming on grass.
Shimmering green and molten gold,
in its allure I stayed awhile.
Dreams I now saw in fair lamplight,
my world I dreamt in fairy glow.
Kissed by magic, I hid that spark
in a glass jar and held it close.
Till I knew that beside my lamp,
the flickering flame would not burn.
The lamp is mine, it shines for me;
it gives light where my feet take me.

My fond star, it shines for the world;
its spry light, but transient charm.
Needing to see, wanting to dream,
I broke my jar and let fire fly.
But this is no end, cannot stop
shadowing incandescent trails.
I must take the arduous road,
a lamp in hand to safely bear.
I must take the arduous road,
a firefly to shelter and care.
I must take the arduous road,
to a place of perpetual light.

5.

Black Like the Flutist

Wafting on the moonbeams
a song
of shadows black
like storm clouds,
deep dark eyes
and fragrant hair,
noisy wings and
cinder yet to burn,
heaving waves on
starless nights,
dark as the future
in longing hearts,
Black like the Flutist
calling to me.

6.

Mundane

While I trudge through swamps of mundane days, my years - they go and quietly hide.

7.

Always June in Kochi

My home still stands pretty
with my folks out front
in the shade of the mango
in that trim little street
that goes nowhere
draped in trees and creepers
where the sunbirds sing
and fruit bats dangle
in the sea sent breeze
while the children play;
But it all seems faded,
tired of waiting.

There's moss on the walls
and waning paint,
There's moss on the mango
wrinkled and dry
with leaves careworn
like those of his parents.

The streets are smooth now,
zippy and zestless
where once they ran
quiet and restless;
The smiles are old
but the faces are new;
The drongos have left
with their racquet tails,
There are no birds to mime
from their breadfruit perch.

But still it rains.
But still it rains
and still it sweats,
It always does at this time,
It always is June here,
I thought those times
had gone for good.

But standing on the street
which goes nowhere,
where still it rains
and still it sweats,
where the sunbirds sing,
where it always is June,
I knew;

I thought those times
had gone for good,
But it was I who left.

8.

From Long Ago

On the gushing streets
where I walk as a stranger
in a stranger land,
in the midst of a crowd
I met an old friend
who beamed at me
from glasses low on the nose
of a face full with time;
All I did was stand and stare.
When my friend patted my arm
and melted away
with a gentler smile,
I said quietly—
You know, it rained that night.

9.

Little Mango Tree

There once was a mango tree
small and sweet in our yard,
it grew under a bigger tree
that towered old and scarred;

It bore a lush ripe mango
red as an apple
but rare as a one man tango,
for all it got was sunny dapple;

We thought him lazy
for the big one filled buckets
while he stood like a daisy
and did nothing but sing with crickets;

Till one day grew a thought -
one tree may bloom with an axe
if the other falls for what it's not;
It broke me when he fell in his tracks.

10.

Old Books

These old books smell of
mildew and times past, pages
yellow with stories
untold and soft with
fingers that turned them.

These old books, they are
like friends we meet long after,
never forgotten,
no distance enough
to stop a warm hug.

11.

Puddle

My school had a puddle
guarding its gates,
it was there before
the school was made
and to this day it makes
every bus moan and creak;
If you stopped by to smile
at the frogs in the mud
the puddle would kindly ask,
Would you like to hop in
to give the frogs a scare?
I'd politely take my shoes off
and say, I better do
Or the next boy will!

12.

Sand

Many years slip away unseen,
like shifting sand beneath my feet.
Can dunes bury all that has been?
Can even time heal those aches sweet?

13.

Stolen

Walk with memories
But watch your step,
Don't hold them so close!
Some are thieves of time
who steal our joys of now,
Some are liars
who make up our past,
Go back and you may find
nothing as you thought it to be.

14.

Where the Light of Delhi Still Burns

Every once in a while I head deep
into the heart of the daunting city
through a maze of streets
narrow and tight, close and bright,
so much so there is no left from right!
Soaked with the noise and scent
of a forgotten world,
of open drains and rotting refuse
of roasting meat and brewing tea
of woody smoke and dirty clothes
of petals sweet and cloying attar,
Shoulders rub at every second feet
brushing shawls and clawing arms,
I feel like a snake freshly sloughed
when I get to the stunted gates,
here where every wish comes true.
Inside here is a world of its own
one that has stood much like this,
a place of peace in an insane world
for a thousand years and a hundred less,
a place of tiles and glittering glass
green and white, gold and rose,

people lost and people sick,
hungry bellies and empty eyes,
people searching for many things;
Inside here everyone is free,
nameless and faceless,
blameless and faithless,
free and quiet as the graves
sixty and five that lie at the feet
of the man who loves them all;
There lie others who walked with him
and chose at the end to sleep with him,
the prince of Persian poetry
a mad cap emperor ever colourful
and a princess long forgotten.
For those that still can't see
the man and his wisdom,
the magic of rough-hewn throats
forged in the fire of endless belief
soars through the night
lighting the way;
And yet,
and yet no woman may go and touch
or honour the man they came to see,
that is now only for their pure men folk;
As I stood drenched in song,
a hand, veined and fair, plucked at my sleeve;
Black drawn the lines of eyes deep and grey
burning with a sorrow that clutched at my heart,
She bade me drape a green silk shawl
for the man who lit the light of Delhi,
a bowl of petals for Hazrat Nizamuddin.

15.

They Grow Old on the Porch

Drip drop
Drip drop,
Rain on the leaves;

Pit pat,
Pit pat,
Rain on the roof;

A chill, a quiet,
A cloud on the wisp
Curling around us;

A rustle, a whistle,
A dancing tree,
A singing thrush;

A hush, a shush,
A pinging void,
Ringing in the ears;

Drip drip,
Drop drop,
We'll keep waiting.

Part-6
Everyday

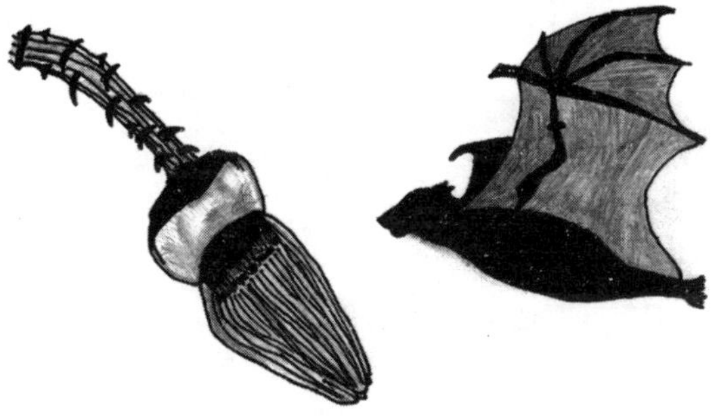

1. ℐ

A Quiet Morning

Such a pleasure waking
from fretful sleep to a placid morning
when the world's quiet and just getting started,
August with trees asleep and light rusted;

The birds are up and dogs about,
there are people walking away from them;
Shutters up and lights are out
and people walking towards them;
Sleepy kids with heavy bags,
Newspapermen and milk vans;

There's a musty hint of last night's drizzle
to go with the high notes of coffee brewing,
The sweet musk of a horse drawn cart
mixed with the rich sappiness of fallen figs;

There's a bell and a horn,
A sprinkle and a pump;
Bits of god and a forgotten tune
seeping through the leaves;

It's a morning like any other,
it's just my mind that's quiet.

2.

Seven

Seven they race
across the pathless
sky of night,
With a load of sun-rays
on a ride endless,
Seven horses bright!

3.

Birds in Their Sky

I looked too long
at the sun and
found myself blind,

I watched birds
in their sky and
found I could fly.

4.

A Smile will Do

All I need
is birdsong
A spot of rain
Trees to sit under
The sound of the sea
Warm food to share
with all my people;
But I'll make do
with a smile
from you.

5.

Busy Bees

While we are busy
looking busy in our suits;
Bees, they make honey.

6.

Go Talk to a Tree

Go talk to a tree
when your days are hard
and sense is a suffering,
When days are withering
and you must water them alone;

Go sit under a rough barked tree
wise beyond your years
and she will tell you
about living in a faraway land
in a strange horde of green,
Of how an errant bolt
cut her head off
and burnt her hollow,
Of how she must carry
ropes on her branch and
stones on her trunk,
Of how her fruits fall unloved
by those on the bench below
who scrawl their love on her;

Go hug a tree standing alone
and he will tell you
the pleasure in letting out
his head to the little folk
for naps and nests,
his friendship with the creeper
flowering on a hairy arm,
Slow, rambling conversations
with queer new friends through
the warm embrace he shares
with rock and soil that hold him up;

Go talk to trees
and they will tell you
to take it slow,
a little bit of rain and
some sun to go with it,
a few kind deeds and
words to bind them with
are all it takes
to grow and grow
beyond these years
and the storms they bring,
Go talk to a tree
and make a friend for life.

7.

I Like to Sit in Parks

On cool clear days
at the fag end of winter
to watch withering leaves
cling tenuously to branches;
Beautiful as they fall,
their flight a reminder
of days red, green and gold;
Some will sleep under their tree
one with its roots,
Others will be swept away
by a careless breeze;
But there is no going back
for any of them
to the heights of the trees
blushing with spring.

8.

My Love, Sleep

I have but one true
love, she with whom every night
I spend in sheer bliss!

What magic she has
in the dark of her tresses,
her embracing warmth!

In her love melts each
tired moment of wakefulness,
all aching muscles.

She is an oracle,
foretelling days unseen and
muddled stories past.

Her words are bitter
for only she sees what lies
within my black heart.

Clocks and maps mean naught -
Into an hour she folds years,
across thoughts, worlds!

Too much of her and
I would be indulgent, too
little brings madness.

Even on nights when
thoughts lead me in endless loops,
she patiently waits.

With her began my
time and with her it must end;
Cannot part, with Sleep.

9.

Beauty

Often, we forget
the beauty around us to
seek it far afield.

10.

Banana Man

For the last ten years
I rush out at noon
from my air-cooled place
to keep myself sane
when I have to go back again,
To have a glass of tea
under the broken tree
while the sun beats down,
On some of those days
while my shoe gets brushed
I sit beside the banana man.
Every day at noon
they are always there
and for the last ten years
seems like nothing has changed
but the date on my page.
Today at noon I had a banana
to go with my shoe
and I saw him again;
He once was old and slim
the banana man,
Now he is gaunt

and barely there,
His cheeks are in
and his hair is thin,
His eyes have dimmed
and his words are slurred,
He just sits there
holding himself,
shivering in the afternoon sun.

11.

Sandhya

A lamp, a pillar of lamps
burning around
A rock cut lord;
A moth, a flicker of moths
Star trailing around
A dying lamp;
A bat, a drunken bat
tripping around
A banana bloom;
A fly, glowing fly
painting around
The gathering gloom;
An ant, a hill of ants
clouding around,
losing their wings.

12.

Solitude, Somewhere Else

In tube-lit halls restless we grow
amidst empty seats glowing low,
They bind us there while in the window sky
the clouds go merrily by
barely seen by those within.

We are the young,
We are those that don't age,
Seems just a day ago that we laughed
through morning and noon
and still we laugh in these halls.

The lights will burn on
while our minds fade out,
Seeking a secret place
where there are no halls and seats,
We are young, we will not sleep here.

Part-7
Folly

1.

People of the Blessed Land

The blessed people lived
in a bountiful land,
a fish-shaped land
hallowed by the sea
and generous peaks,
with plentiful rivers,
a treasure of green
and rain, blissful rain!

Half of the people
owed it to god
while the rest trusted in
the power of people,
So blessed they felt
they all agreed
it is a land of gods;
So blessed they felt
they grew rich and happy
and marched onward
but forgot their blessing.

The sea frowned at them
and sent forth her clouds,
it rained
and they walked in it
to wash away their sweat;
it rained again
steadily now,
and they brought out their umbrellas;

it rained again
with furrowed brow this time,
they smiled and went on with their lives;
it rained again
harder still,
they smiled and splashed to work;
it rained again
with purpose now,
they laughed and raced boats in the streets;
they laughed and still did not remember.

They laughed and said,
we have tamed the rivers
and walled them in,
we have tamed the forests
and our gods live in the hills,
we have tamed the land
and our crops are gold,
we have bridges and boats
and our homes are brick & mortar;
the sea is our mother,
she will swallow anything
you throw at us
and we throw out,
and they laughed
and went back to work.

The rain called her allies
and went to her mountains
where their first-born
river and forest grow,
she called and they came;
It rained then,
it rained and rained
from the sea to the mountains;
Thunder lent the rivers his hammer
The mountains gave them his might
The clouds became their darkness
and the sea filled them with her rage;

Down came the rivers,
the forests parted to
let them pass
and then trampled their roads;
Down came the rivers,
red and rocky with rage
drowning their shrines,
burying their green;
Down came the rivers
smashing the walls that hemmed them in,
bursting the banks that they chose to keep,
cutting through their paper houses
and stacks of silly towns;
It rained and rained
till the once blessed people
called upon the sea,
But she only howled,
swollen with fury
and blew them a swirling gust;

It rained and rained
till each mountain was an island,
till each city was mud,
till their bridges swam,
till their boats climbed trees,
till they were wet to their bones,
till they no longer laughed,
till they fell to their knees
and remembered
that they once were blessed;
and the sea said,
it's time to learn
to walk in the rain again.

2.

Rain Trees

Do rain-trees grow
where it rains?
Or
Does it rain
where rain-trees grow?

3.

More Than You Know

Do you know me, sir?
I speak not of the colour
of my face and hair.

Do you know me, sir?
No, not by the tongue I speak
Or where I am from.

Do you know me, sir?
I meant not the name of my
God or what I eat.

Do you know me, sir?
Not by where I live and work,
Or my golden hoard.

Do you know me, sir?
Ask not how loud I talk,
Or by my love of stage.

Do you know me, sir?
Not by how much I know or
how fast I can run.

Do you know me, sir?
Never by what you think of
my man-woman-hood.

If you think you know—
This is but a bit, I am
more than all of these.

Know me when my heart
is in what I say and do;
By the paths I take.

I am how I treat
the old and poor, weak and meek,
And other men's faith.

Know by how I let
my friends and better half fly;
By my dear folk's pride.

Read me from thoughts in
my head, the flowers I smell;
By how I know you.

If you still must know,
We are all rivers that must
once end in the sea.

4.

Those That We Call Mother

Dip by dip she
washes our sins,
Drip by drip we
poison her soul.

Drop by drop she
fills our bellies,
Bit by bit we
steal her life.

Leaf by leaf she
grows our world,
Yard by yard we
tear her apart.

Brick by brick she
built our lives,
Day by day we
leave her alone.

Step by step she
walks beside us,
Prick by prick we
bleed her more.

Why do we not
see what we do
to those who
we call Mother?

5.

Men of This World

Men of this world,
we are but fools!
Honour we seek and
of love we sing,
Parity we crave and
for freedom we cry;
To what end such
passion, if only for self?
Remember what we do to
the bird we treasure
for its lilting song and
wondrous flight.
Men of the world
in all our folly,
we promise haven and
fancy it lies in a cage!
Awhile the bird may sing
under the taunting sky,
but not for long for
Men of this World.

6.

If Milk Ran Red

Fowls in their coop,
Goats to the slaughter,
Dirty hogs and sacred cows;
Our eyes tear for them,
Our hearts cry for them!
Lush green paddy ripe to be reaped,
Mother and calf and their stolen milk,
Tall old trees lopped for our beds,
What fond smiles they bring to our lips!
If only the trees would scream,
If only her milk ran red.

7.

This Glass Cage

I toil in this long room
With wide screens and white walls,
Shiny floors and polished people.
All they talk is of plants & time,
Ticking clocks and
Monsters belching smoke.
When I look for stars,
All I see are hawkers
and lucre their only wonder.
Cold air is everywhere and yet
my head is hot, and I yearn
to be out gulping hazy air.
Free your mind and
think out-of-box, they say;
Surely, they know this is a cage!

9.

Hollow

What lies we speak to hide
the truth in our hearts!
What questions we ask to mask
the answers on our tongue!

10.

Along came an Empire

We chased off old King-in-name
who let his men loot our
hard-earned wealth and sense,
an all-seeing man whose
silence was deafening.

We love our new Emperor
who let his men steal our
pride and fragile quiet,
a loud man of many words that
say as much as old King-in-name.

11.

Sculptor

I will make you
from stone and heart,
with mallet and chisel;

When it is done
I will still be man but
You will be a god.

Fear no doubts
And poisoned words,
I will keep you safe.

12.

Weeds

When morning came bright,
the farmer cut down some weeds
with his sweeping blade.

The child came for her
wee blue flowers and found them
all dead in a pile.

13.

Beyond

It is indeed odd that we fear
old Death and his sister Change
until our reckoning,
When nothing is ordained
but these dire siblings,
everything else is
just a falling raindrop.
When rivers change course,
it is not the end of their ebb,
their flow still heals
beyond their curves.
We may yet feed the earth
when we are all gone,
Nature may yet be reborn,
Our world sees new dawns.

14.

Yamuna Goes to Allahabad

Standing on the steps
of yesterday's ashes
I saw her come slow
under the cold iron bridge;
What began as
a melting piece of ice
tumbling blue down the hills
in a giggle of silt and foam,
Strolling through the flats
with broken dreams and branches,
limps into this city
to drink the poison of our world
and carry a flood of black souls
east to the holy junction
to meet a greater sister
dying from her burden.

15.

Conquest

On the peak I screamed
into the whistling wind
and marched back to camp
with the sun's glow in me;
I strode to the fire
where my wrinkled guide stretched
and said, It is done now,
That mountain is mine!
He looked past me and
shook his head with a smile.
I turned around to see
what he saw –
Still and sombre, the mountain stood,
Just as it was, just as it will,
my trampling feet gone long ago;
While here I stand
feeling just a little lost,
for the mountain fills my heart.

Part-8

A Window Within

1.

Grandmother's Stories

My grandmother
was just like yours,
soft and nice, gentle and wise;
She made me things
and bade me sleep,
She told me stories
about gods and men.

She told me about
Rama of the Bow
who was a bit of God
but still had need
of one brave brother
and an army of friends
to slay his demons;
She told me of
Rama of the Bow
who was just a silly man
when he let Sita go;
Sita, who bore it all,
and grew stronger still;
The city that laughed at

a monkey for his tail
and got burnt down,
The meek palm squirrel
who helped build
the bridge across the sea.

She told me of
the first great war
where brothers killed brothers
for fame and land
and none was a hero;
She wept most
for the Sun god's son
who gave away his might
but still turned up to fight;
She loved best
the son of Dharma,
a man who lost all
to a throw of dice,
for he walked with his dog
to the cold bitter end.

She told me of
great King Bali
and his big fat belly,
whose goodwill made
the gods envious,
who gave his life
to a tiny god
to keep his word,
a man whose deeds
made him dearer than god.

Later when she thought
I'd grown out of stories
she told me this:
I don't care whether
you grow rich or poor,
I don't care whether
you grow great
or die obscure
but know this well;
Be as kind as you can be
to one and all,
Give what you can
to those in need,
Don't laugh too hard
or cry too loud,
Do your best
and then let it be
for trust is worth more
than love ever will be,
Water your plants
and clean your desk,
Learn from your teachers
and hold them close,
Learn from your parents
for they are the best you have,
Love them dear
but don't walk like them
for you are another
and need to go elsewhere.

2.

A Moment

Savour still silence
amidst mad clamour,
Would stars be pretty
without black between?

It takes but a wink
to taste new flowers,
Flitting about on
frail butterfly wings.

3.

Clouded

Wipe away the mist,
Look out of the window to
Find what lies within.

4.

A Flower's Will

A time to smile and bloom,
A time to wither and die;
The fragrance between is
the flower's own will.

5.

Talking of Hope

We sat on the rock
side by side with
our feet in the grass,
waiting.
I was there for the
wild ones that come
to quench their thirst
before the sun slept red.
She sat there close
looking at nothing
in the still green water,
I did not know why.
And then she asked,
What is this Hope?
But I knew less
than she ever would.
So I told her instead
about the leopard
that haunts this place,
a remarkable beast.

Beautiful and elusive,
he comes and goes
yet no one knows
if he is just a rumour
hunting in the hills
and walking the night.
I know well his wet track
padding up the stream
but never saw him once.
Maybe it is better
to not get close
for it is in his paws
to strike us dead.
She looked at me strange
and said soft,
you don't know
and you never will.

6. How

In stone, in metal,
I see you everywhere; will
I know when we meet?

7.

A Rough Sea

I can't stem the rot,
can't blame the mob
or nip rumours in their bud,
What I can do is
keep walking my way
and stand up for right!

I can't stop the storm,
can't tame the waves
or turn the gale around,
What I can do is
point the sail my way
and hold on tight!

9.

Lamp-Lit

Where veils are thick
as velvet
there is no wit;
Draw them aside—
No oil, no wick,
and yet
the lamp is lit.

10.

What Will I Be

Before I knew how
to lace my shoes
I was asked,
What will you be?
I wasn't sure
and so was told,
what I should be.
Many rains have
come and gone but
what I didn't know then
I still don't know.
But now, I know for sure
what no one asked—
What I cannot be and
don't ever want to be.

11.

Funny Bones

Have you seen a skull
that frowns and sulks?
All they ever do
is grin and smirk!
If it's all so funny
when we are but bones,
why should we worry
when we are so much more!

12.

Within

I ran and ran
and then some more
down dark alleys
chasing tranquil light
till I could no more.
There in the dark
with nowhere to go,
standing still and
breathing slow,
I found it within.

13.

Grumpy

Every day I do
things that don't need doing
and don't like done;
Every day I rush
things that need no hurrying
and see no point in;
Every day I say
things that don't need saying
and do no good;
Every day I find
things to tell others
about why I don't smile more.

14.

A Herd Comes Home

Quietly came a lonesome tune
straggling through the broken dunes
tired at the heels of a weary day
stretched in to the corners
of a fading sky by silent crows;
Nothing moved in the empty place
till there came a cloud of fallen rays
rumbling through the prickly scrub
filled with horns and hooves
swaying to that sandy tune;
In their midst a shadow striding
in the gold of dusk her cape flying
walking them from out of the sun,
They follow where she goes
And her song written in dust.

Other #SM Poetry Books